Be Kind to One Another

The Inspiring Journey of Ellen DeGeneres

(An Unauthorized Biography)

By

Bertrand Fon

Copyright © 2024 by Bertrand Fon

All rights reserved.

No part of this publication may be reproduced, distributed, or transmitted in any form or by any means, including photocopying, recording, or other electronic or mechanical methods, or by any information storage and retrieval system without the prior written permission of the publisher, except in very brief quotations embodied in critical reviews and certain other noncommercial uses allowed by copyright law.

ISBN: 979-8-9895178-0-0 (Paperback)

Front & Back Cover Photographs: Getty Images (https://www.gettyimages.com/)

Dedication

It is hard to say thanks when there are so many people to thank. To my wife and life partner, Rita, from the bottom of my heart, I thank you. I couldn't have done this without your unconditional love and support.

I am beyond grateful to my family, especially my parents and siblings (Dr and Mrs. Chimangha, Valentine, Diana, Nina & Carlson). There are not enough words to express my appreciation; all the tea in China is not enough to express how grateful I am, fam.

Thanks to the United States Army for the opportunity to serve; the Army values **(Loyalty, Duty, Respect, Selfless Service, Honor, Integrity, and Personal Courage)** changed my life so profoundly; I couldn't imagine a more incredible honor.

Thanks to all the service men and women, active and retired, and their families (Army, Marine Corps, Navy, Air Force, Space Force, Coast Guard, Veteran); your dedication, sacrifice, support, and everything makes life worthwhile. America and its people would never be the same without you.

Finally, I dedicate this book to Ellen. I have watched her show since I came to the US a decade ago; it has been inspirational and life changing.

Dear Ellen,

I watched your uplifting show religiously with all the great content and amazing guests, and it became part of my life right up to the season finale. Your life journey, personality, humbleness, uniqueness, and everything inspires me. Your mantra: "Be kind to one another," now helps me to give and forgive myself and others more easily. Being an immigrant, watching the show also helped me improve my English language.

I am writing this book to celebrate, honor, and appreciate you. Thanks for all the laughs, quizzes, pranks, life lessons, kindness, energy, fun, joy, creativity, countless memories, kind words, and viral moments your show created. I miss the Halloween specials. Watching your show live in the studio and meeting you in person was on my bucket list, but I am glad I watched it on TV. I hope I will meet you in person one day.

You paved the way for many to break out of their shells and live their truth. You also made me more open and respectful of other people's choices. You are a class act and legend of daytime television who makes the world better. I wish you and Portia the best in all your current and future undertakings. No one is more deserving.

    Thanks for everything, and God Bless you!

LEGAL & DISCLAIMER

This book is an unauthorized biography of Ellen DeGeneres. It is intended to be an informative and engaging account of her life and work. The author has made every effort to ensure the accuracy of the information presented in this book. However, the author does not guarantee the accuracy or completeness of any information contained herein. The book is not intended to be a definitive or exhaustive account of Ellen DeGeneres' life and career. It is simply one person's perspective on her life and work. However, I cannot guarantee that there are no omissions.

The author disclaims any liability for any damage resulting from the use of information contained in this book. The content and information in this book are intended for informational, educational and inspirational purposes only. All proceeds from this book will be used for charitable and non-profit purposes only.

I hope you enjoy the book!

Table of Contents

Dedication III
LEGAL & DISCLAIMER V
INTRODUCTION 1
CHAPTER 1 3
STARDUST & SHADOW 3
CHAPTER 2 8
THE FLIGHT OF A STAR 8
CHAPTER 3 15
INSIDE THE WHIRLWIND 15
CHAPTER 4 24
THE COMEDIC CHAMELEON 24
CHAPTER 5 28
THE WALTZ OF LOVE AND TABOOS IN HOLLYWOOD 28
CHAPTER 6 32
A RAINBOW REVOLUTION 32
CHAPTER 7 37
THE UNFURLING OF AN ENCHANTING EMPIRE 37
CHAPTER 8 45
A DANCE OF BENEVOLENCE AND LAUGHTER 45
Chapter 9: The Power of Positivity 57
CHAPTER 10 64
THE LEGACY AND LESSONS CARVED BY ELLEN DEGENERES 64
45 QUOTES BY ELLEN 71
REFERENCES 78

INTRODUCTION

From her modest beginnings in Louisiana, Ellen DeGeneres was always poised to enchant the world with her wit and influence. Growing up, she boldly embraced her identity as a gay woman, choosing authenticity over conformity. Her journey took her to Los Angeles, where she shattered societal norms by publicly coming out on her sitcom, "Ellen." Despite facing backlash, her resolve never wavered, and she stood as a beacon of boundless love and fearless individuality.

In 2003, "The Ellen DeGeneres Show" burst onto the scene, transforming the landscape of talk shows with its mix of deep conversations, laughter, and celebrity charm. Even amidst controversy over workplace culture, Ellen's spirit remained unbroken, continuously captivating her audience. Her show was packed with memorable catchphrases and viral moments, like the iconic Oscars selfie, cementing her status as a pop culture icon.

Ellen is more than just a comedian or celebrity; she's a trailblazer who has imprinted the world with her unique blend of authenticity, resilience, and humor. This book takes you on a journey through her compelling story, uncovering the essence that has made her a beloved figure in culture.

Through interviews, personal anecdotes, and exclusive glimpses behind the scenes, we invite readers to discover the extraordinary path Ellen has traveled, from her early days to her ascent to global recognition. Step into the world of Ellen DeGeneres, where sincerity reigns supreme and delightful surprises await.

CHAPTER 1
STARDUST & SHADOW

In a land caressed by sunshine, where cicadas orchestrated the air and magnolia trees shared whispered secrets, a legend emerged beneath the Louisiana sky. This is the enchanting story of Ellen DeGeneres, a radiant beacon destined to scatter the darkness with her sparkling laughter, endless empathy, and undaunted spirit. Her journey began in Metairie, Louisiana, on January 26, 1958, setting the stage for an extraordinary life.

Ellen's roots were modest—born to an insurance salesman with dreams tucked into his pockets and a speech therapist mother whose words could mend the most profound silences. However, her world shifted as her parents' marriage dissolved during her pivotal teenage years. Ellen, whose dreams spanned the skies, initially aspired to heal animals. Yet, she found the academic world restrictive, like chains binding her dreams. "I'm not book smart," she confided in the stars, little knowing her true path would weave through diverse experiences, from waiting tables to painting houses, each step an integral move towards her fate.

At 28, Ellen DeGeneres stood under the harsh glare of public speaking, her every nerve screaming with stage fright. Yet, in an unexpected twist, she transformed her jittery nerves into waves of laughter, creating an unforgettable connection with her audience. It was a magical moment, a mere hint of the incredible journey she was about to embark on.

Ellen was cradled in the principles of Christian Science, her youth a tapestry of Sunday sermons and the heart-stirring rhythms of gospel music. However, as she grew, a storm of questions began to brew within her, signaling a future where she would emerge as a luminary for advocacy and equality, especially for the LGBTQ+ community.

Her life's story took a dramatic turn following her parents' divorce when she was just 16. Moving to Atlanta, Texas, marked the beginning of a new era where Ellen would craft her unique symphony of laughter and resilience, weaving her narrative with threads of change and becoming a global icon of hope and joy.

Ellen DeGeneres' educational odyssey began at Atlanta High School before she returned to the lively ambiance of New Orleans, immersing herself in communication studies at the University of New Orleans. Yet, the structured confines of academia couldn't hold her boundless spirit. She embarked on a journey through a kaleidoscope of jobs, each one adding a unique stroke to her life's rich tapestry.

Ellen's name resonates through time, leaving an indelible mark on countless hearts. As a comedian, television host, actress, and writer, she embodies the essence of humor, courage, and advocacy. Her narrative champions the power of laughter to light up the darkness, bravery to face the night, and a steadfast voice that champions those lurking in the shadows.

Her saga, punctuated by joyful laughter, unwavering courage, and tireless advocacy, continues to enchant and inspire people worldwide, painting her as an enduring beacon of hope and joy in the tapestry of human experience.

Her father, Elliot, a man of faith and foresight, and her mother, Elizabeth, a woman whose heritage was as rich as her spirit, provided the foundation upon which Ellen built her dreams. Ellen's brother, Vance DeGeneres, shared the artistic flame that burned within her; his life was a tapestry of creativity and service. The story of their family, marked by love, loss, and laughter, is a testament to the indomitable spirit of the human heart.

In the shadow of her parents' parting, Ellen and her mother sought refuge in the arms of Atlanta, Texas. It was here, amid the echoes of her mother's challenges, that Ellen's light began to shine brightest, her humor a beacon in the night. This period marked the dawn of Ellen's journey towards

Throughout her formative years, Ellen DeGeneres encountered pivotal experiences that not only shaped her personal evolution but also steered her towards a life filled with purpose, creativity, and significant social influence. These moments weren't mere stepping stones in her journey but profound catalysts for change, guiding her path in remarkable ways.

A cornerstone experience for Ellen was her deep dive into volunteer work. Through her involvement with communities grappling with socioeconomic hardships, Ellen came face-to-face with realities starkly different from her own. This engagement in varied environments broadened her perspective, unveiling the intricate layers of social issues and the systemic roots of inequality.

Such interactions didn't just expand Ellen's worldview; they ignited a passion within her to use her platform for advocacy and change.

This chapter in her life laid the groundwork for her future endeavors, where she would leverage her voice, humor, and influence to shed light on issues close to her heart and make a tangible impact on society.

It was during these volunteer missions that Ellen learned the importance of empathy, humility, and listening to the community's voice. The realization that real change requires participatory solutions informed much of her later work, driving her to develop initiatives that were not only innovative but also inclusive and empowering for those they sought to assist.

Ellen's adolescence was also marked by a voracious appetite for knowledge. She was known to spend hours in libraries, absorbing everything from classical literature to contemporary scientific research. This period of intense academic exploration was crucial in shaping her interdisciplinary approach to problem-solving. She developed an ability to draw connections between seemingly unrelated fields. This skill would become a signature of her later work. Ellen's academic curiosity led her to pursue advanced studies in her chosen field, where she challenged conventional wisdom and explored new paradigms. This intellectual bravery, cultivated during her youth, equipped her with the critical thinking skills necessary to innovate and lead in her profession.

Another defining experience of Ellen's young adulthood was her leadership role in a multidisciplinary team project aimed at addressing a global challenge. Along with leading a diverse group of peers, Ellen honed her teamwork, communication, and project management skills.

Ellen's adventure shines a spotlight on the magic of teamwork and the beauty of diverse minds working together to hatch brilliant solutions. It planted in her a deep-rooted belief in the wonders of joining forces across fields, cultures, and backgrounds. The triumph of her project, along with the accolades gathered, didn't just boost her confidence; it solidified her drive to forge a career dedicated to sparking positive change in society.

But Ellen's path was speckled with obstacles. From the pressure to excel academically to bumps in her project and the juggle between her dreams and personal life, Ellen faced it all. Yet, each hurdle brought with it a lesson in grit and self-care.

These hurdles weren't just obstacles; they were stepping stones. They taught Ellen to be fluid, to reflect, and to find the sweet spot between chasing her professional dreams and cherishing her personal life. This journey of growth transformed her into a resilient leader, ready to tackle any challenge with elegance and resolve.

CHAPTER 2
THE FLIGHT OF A STAR

At the tender age of twenty-three, Ellen DeGeneres stood at a pivotal crossroads, unaware that her path was set to sparkle with laughter and light. Her comedic genius didn't first glimmer under the grand spotlight or on a grand stage but shone during intimate gatherings with close friends. These early supporters saw the brilliance in Ellen's humor, recognizing it as a rare gem that deserved a wider audience. Their genuine, infectious laughter became the chorus that propelled Ellen to share her unique take on life with more people.

Ellen's formative years were steeped in the rich tapestry of New Orleans—a city pulsating with life, rhythm, and soul. This vibrant backdrop served as the perfect playground for her burgeoning imagination. Ellen reminisced about these times in an interview with Liz Scott of New Orleans Magazine, sharing, "I rode my bike everywhere... New Orleans is a really special place." Her words echo the profound influence her hometown had on her spirit, highlighting the city's unique charm and vibrancy.

However, the melody of Ellen's life took a somber turn with her parents' divorce when she was just thirteen, an event that uprooted her and her mother, leading them to Atlanta, Texas. The move marked a stark departure from the lively streets of New Orleans. Amidst this upheaval, Ellen discovered her ability to use humor as a beacon of hope, a tool not just for her own coping but also for bringing light to those around her.

This realization marked the beginning of Ellen's journey to becoming a beacon of humor and resilience, using her gift to navigate and illuminate the darker moments of life.

Ellen's talent for comedic mimicry and jests became a beacon of light for her mother, lifting her from despair to joyous laughter. This transformative power of comedy, an act of love and resilience, underscored the profound impact humor can have on our lives. Buoyed by her friends' steadfast belief in her extraordinary gift, Ellen was inspired to step out from the cozy gatherings and onto the stages of local coffee shops and comedy clubs. These early forays into the public eye served as a crucible, shaping and refining her comedic identity.

Ellen's relatable, heartfelt humor resonated deeply with audiences, her stories and reflections mirroring the universal truths of the human condition. Her connection with the audience grew with each performance, as did her confidence. This marked the onset of Ellen's meteoric rise from the intimate circles of friendly laughter to captivating a global audience, reshaping the comedy landscape with her distinctive voice and vision. Ellen's journey from those early days of tentative steps onto small stages to becoming a beloved comedy icon illustrates the power of believing in one's unique talents and the transformative potential of sharing those gifts with the world.

Ellen found her rhythm on the comedy stage, her style characterized by a delightful simplicity. She shunned controversial topics and gender-specific humor, striving to craft jokes that everyone could enjoy.

In 1982, Ellen's comedic genius transcended the borders of New Orleans and propelled her to national fame. Winning a talent show competition sponsored by the Cable Network Showtime, she received the honorary title "Funniest Person in America." This accolade opened the doors to perform stand-up comedy on the national stage, a platform that let her tickle the funny bones of audiences across the country.

The year 1986 marked a significant milestone in Ellen's comedy career. Johnny Carson, the stalwart of late-night television, invited Ellen to perform on "The Tonight Show." This was no ordinary invitation, for the show's tradition was that comedians would perform their act and then exit the stage without sharing a conversation with Carson live on camera. However, Ellen's performance was so captivating that it carved a path straight to the coveted sofa. She was the first female comedian to be offered this honor.

In 1991, at the pinnacle of her stand-up career, Ellen DeGeneres was honored as the best female stand-up comic at the American Comedy Awards. Amid the accolades and laughter, she stood on the brink of embarking on a new venture—acting.

Ellen DeGeneres's foray into series television narrates a story of perseverance and pioneering achievements, characterized by initial challenges and subsequent victories. During the late '80s and early '90s, DeGeneres ventured into sitcoms, with brief roles in "Open House" (1989) and "Laurie Hill" (1992). However, these shows failed to resonate with audiences.

Her early acting endeavors led to short-lived sitcoms until 1994, when she starred in "These Friends of Mine," portraying Ellen Morgan. The sitcom, which celebrated the humor found in everyday life, quickly gained popularity due to Ellen's unique humor and relatable character. Acknowledging the show's growing appeal, its name was changed to "Ellen" from the second season onwards. DeGeneres's performance was critically acclaimed, earning her multiple Emmy nominations and a Peabody Award in 1997.

However, in the spring of 1997, Ellen made television history in a profoundly personal way.

Ellen, who had until then kept her sexuality a private matter known only to her close circle, began to hint at her sexual orientation through her comedy. In one memorable scene, she emerges from a closet, joking, "Sorry, I was in the closet." Such lines led to speculation about her sexuality among her audience. Ultimately, she courageously revealed that she was gay, both off-screen and through her character on the show, marking a significant moment in television history.

In an episode titled "The Puppy Episode," her character came out as a lesbian, marking a historic moment as the first openly gay main character on a network sitcom. This revelation not only shattered stereotypes but also broke significant barriers in the television industry. Concurrently, Ellen publicly came out through a Time magazine cover story, mirroring her character's brave declaration.

The announcement triggered a vast array of reactions. While many fans sent letters of support, applauding her honesty, others reacted with shock, and a controversy ensued. As a result, the show suffered a loss of viewership and a decline in ratings and eventually found itself on unstable ground.

Advertisers withdrew, influenced by the controversy, and the network began to issue warning labels on episodes that depicted Ellen's sexuality.

The 1997-98 season proved tumultuous, leading to the show's cancellation. Despite these challenges, Ellen exemplified resilience and authenticity, igniting conversations that would influence television for years to come.

Post-cancellation, Ellen navigated a difficult period both professionally and personally, marked by her high-profile breakup with actress Anne

Heche in August 2000 and an unsuccessful venture into film with roles in "EDtv" and "The Love Letter." Although critically acclaimed, a subsequent sitcom in 2001, "The Ellen Show," failed to attract a significant audience.

However, Ellen's career was far from over. The aftermath of the 9/11 attacks presented an unexpected opportunity when she was chosen to host the twice-postponed Primetime Emmy Awards. Her adept handling of the event, characterized by a perfect blend of humor and respect, offered solace and entertainment to viewers and peers alike.

Ellen's return to the television limelight included hosting Saturday Night Live, guest-starring on Will & Grace, and featuring in Hollywood Squares. In 2003, she returned to stand-up comedy, embarking on a successful thirty-five-city tour that culminated in an HBO special, "Ellen DeGeneres: Here and Now."

Her foray into literature with a book of comedic essays and her voice role as Dory in "Finding Nemo" further solidified her comeback. Ellen's voice performance was particularly notable for its warmth and relatability, which endeared her to worldwide audiences.

With her unwavering spirit and distinctive charm, Ellen DeGeneres ventured into a new domain in 2003, transforming the landscape of daytime television with the launch of her own talk show. This wasn't just another program added to the roster; it was a revelation, a fresh wave of humor, humanity, and humility that set Ellen apart from the myriad hosts vying for attention. With her unique blend of light-heartedness and sincerity, she created an environment where audiences didn't just watch the show; they became a part of it, often joining in the dance, echoing the show's underlying message of joy and inclusivity.

The acclaim was swift and resounding. Ellen's daytime talk show became a cultural phenomenon, earning her multiple Emmy nominations and securing the prestigious "Best Talk Show" award. This wasn't merely a win for the show; it was a testament to Ellen's profound impact on television and her personal fulfillment in her work. She wasn't just hosting a show; she was reshaping the very fabric of daytime TV with her authenticity and approachability.

Ellen's influence extended beyond the confines of her studio. In a world obsessed with rigid beauty standards, she stood as a beacon of authenticity, embracing her true self and, in doing so, empowering young women everywhere to do the same. Her style, demeanor, openness—every facet of Ellen resonated with those seeking a figure of genuine substance in a sea of superficiality.

Off the camera, Ellen found solace and joy in her personal life with her partner, Alexandra Hedison.

Together, they built a serene existence away from the glitz and glamour of Hollywood in the tranquil hills that offered a sanctuary from the bustling world below.

Ellen's journey, marked by laughter, resilience, and love, continues to inspire and captivate, proving that true happiness begins with living authentically and spreading joy to others.

Ellen's journey underscores the power of staying true to oneself in a world that often demands conformity. Through her digital presence, she continues to share laughter, emotion, and wisdom, challenging societal norms and promoting inclusivity. Her vibrant personality and openness about her experiences as a gay woman have made her a pivotal figure in the LGBTQ+ community, creating a space filled with humor, grace, and joy.

Her show stands out for its entertainment value and message of self-acceptance. It educates, enlightens, and inspires, encouraging critical thought among viewers. Ellen's stage is the world, and her audience continues to grow. She entertains while addressing important topics, leaving a lasting impact on her viewers.

The most liberating and powerful mantra at the heart of Ellen's philosophy: Be yourself. This credo, reverberating in her every action, every joke, and every dance, has made her a compelling advocate for self-expression and acceptance. As she shines her light on homosexuality and self-love, Ellen emerges as a crucial figure in our society's ongoing discourse of acceptance and change. She's a role model for the ages.

CHAPTER 3
INSIDE THE WHIRLWIND

On September 8, 2003, daytime TV was forever changed with the launch of "The Ellen DeGeneres Show." Right off the bat, it shone as a dazzling gem among the usual daytime offerings. With her unmatched humor and heart, Ellen DeGeneres flipped the talk show script into a joyous celebration of life's colorful tapestry. The show quickly became a cultural hotspot, mixing celebrity chats, live music, and heartfelt stories into an irresistible blend.

Ellen's signature wit and her real interest in her guests' tales not only built a devoted audience but also bagged the show a jaw-dropping 64 Daytime Emmy Awards. These weren't just nods to the show's fun factor but a salute to its soulful connection with viewers and its knack for touching lives deeply.

As the years rolled by, "The Ellen DeGeneres Show" evolved into more than just a source of entertainment; it became a beacon of kindness, mirroring Ellen's own life mantra: "Be kind to one another." This powerful, simple message pulsed through the show's veins, inspiring viewers far and wide. Ellen and her crew dedicated themselves to spreading this positive vibe, reminding us of the magic kindness holds in brightening a sometimes dim world.

The show's allure was magnified by the galaxy of stars that graced its stage, turning each episode into a celebration of human achievement and creativity. Silver screen icons, musical geniuses, champions of sport, and political visionaries all found a place on Ellen's couch, sharing their stories and talents with the world.

This kaleidoscope of guests not only entertained but inspired, making "The Ellen DeGeneres Show" a beacon for those seeking to make a positive impact in their own lives and the lives of others.

As "The Ellen DeGeneres Show" continued to evolve, it became more than a staple of daytime television; it became a movement, a community united by the joy of laughter and the strength of kindness. Ellen's unwavering commitment to spreading positivity has left an indelible mark on the hearts of millions, proving that television can be a powerful force for good in the world.

- **Jennifer Aniston**

This is one name that shines particularly brightly among these celestial guests. Aniston, the beloved Hollywood actress, was the maiden guest to add her sparkle to "The Ellen DeGeneres Show." In its debut episode, she stood by Ellen, who was her close friend.

Jennifer Aniston, already a household name due to her unforgettable portrayal of the ever-lovable Rachel Green in "Friends," added another layer of allure to the first episode of Ellen's show. The stage was set, the lights dimmed, and the applause thundered through the studio as Aniston's radiant smile lit up the stage.

It was a greeting not merely between a host and her guest but an exchange imbued with the warmth of deep, off-screen friendship.

The conversation flowed, brimming with stories, wisecracks, and infectious laughter, particularly during the reminiscence of Ellen's cameo in "Friends."

The energy between Aniston's bubbling charm and Ellen's comic finesse was so captivating not only due to Aniston's star value but also stood as a testament to Ellen's commitment to real connections, loyalty, and friendship.

- **Kanye West**

As "The Ellen DeGeneres Show" played on, an electrifying encounter soon followed, leaving audiences both awestruck and intrigued. The stage was about to be graced by a tour-de-force of the entertainment industry—the enigmatic and multi-talented Kanye West.

West's larger-than-life persona and Ellen's charismatic stage presence resulted in an unforgettable episode. As a rapper, producer, and fashion mogul, Kanye West's appearance on the show would spotlight his creative genius, unique perspectives, and flair for enthralling conversations.

True to his unwavering authenticity, West did not tiptoe around societal hurdles. His candid conversation ventured into the uncharted territories of racism, mental health, and the essence of creative freedom. His views, as provocative as they were poignant, disrupted the status quo, triggering dialogues that rippled beyond the studio, pushing viewers to question and contemplate the world they inhabit.

The heartfelt exchange between West and Ellen let the audience experience a depth and connection that transcended typical celebrity interviews.

The Aftershock: Kanye West's seismic visit to "The Ellen DeGeneres Show" reverberated globally, reaching millions of viewers. It served as a stark reminder that influential figures in the entertainment industry could propel dialogue that contributes to larger societal discourses.

- **Barack Obama**

The air buzzed with excitement as "The Ellen DeGeneres Show" rolled out the red carpet for an exceptional visitor—Barack Obama. The meeting of these two powerhouses, each with a deep-rooted drive to effect positive change, was nothing short of electric. Together, Ellen and Obama delivered a masterclass in charm and wisdom.

Their conversation danced effortlessly between playful jests and profound discussions. Ellen's adept interviewing unlocked a treasure trove of insights from Obama, spanning heartfelt personal anecdotes, reflections on his presidential legacy, and visions for his future projects.

They navigated through a wide array of critical issues—public service, climate action, equality, and the transformative power of empathy—making for an unforgettable exchange that was both enlightening and entertaining.

Advocacy Amplified: During his appearance on "The Ellen DeGeneres Show," Barack Obama, a dedicated advocate for many social causes, used the influential platform to raise awareness about important issues close to his heart.

He seized the opportunity to discuss his foundation's initiatives, including expanding access to education, empowering young leaders, and advocating for healthcare reforms. By highlighting these efforts, he inspired viewers to act and become catalysts for positive change within their communities.

A Meeting of Mirth: Both Barack Obama and Ellen DeGeneres are renowned for their innate wit and infectious humor, infusing their interaction with a sparkling blend of rib-tickling exchanges and playful jests. Their shared humor served as a unifying thread, dissolving the intensity of grave discussions and forging a personal connection with the audience. The episode's lighthearted banter and comedic repartees rendered it a uniquely informative and entertaining spectacle.

Messages of Motivation: Obama's words echoed with a powerful resonance, instilling encouragement and inspiration in the viewers. His eloquent wisdom and ability to distill complex ideas into relatable narratives empowered individuals to believe in their capacity to drive change. His visit to "The Ellen DeGeneres Show" resonated with the message that each person holds the potential to make a difference and that collective action can catalyze societal transformation.

Legacy and Impact: Obama's appearance on "The Ellen DeGeneres Show" left a lasting impression, symbolizing the power of meaningful conversation and accentuating the importance of using influential platforms for impactful dialogues. The episode stirred viewers to practice empathy, commit to social causes, and strive for an inclusive and compassionate society.

- **Rihanna**

Ellen introduced Rihanna, highlighting her journey in music, fashion, and beauty. They discussed Rihanna's recent music projects, her philanthropic endeavors, and her vision of inclusivity.

The episode included a playful game segment, and Rihanna delivered a heartfelt monologue about positive influence and individuality.

- **Steve Harvey**

Steve Harvey, a television powerhouse, ventured into Ellen's domain, each bringing their signature mix of humor, charisma, and honesty to the forefront. From the get-go, Ellen and Steve ignited the stage with their dynamic rapport, sparking laughter and admiration in equal measure.

Their dialogue took a captivating journey through Steve's storied career, offering the audience a glimpse of the person behind the iconic smile. Known for their commitment to making the world a better place, Ellen and Steve delved deep into their charitable work.

They shone a light on the power of kindness, their passion for giving back echoing in their discussion. This wasn't just a chat; it was an inspiration, a rallying cry for everyone watching to play their part in spreading positivity and generosity. Ellen and Steve, through their lively exchange, reminded us all of the impact we can have by simply aiming to improve our little slice of the world.

- **David Beckham**

The day had arrived: The legendary David Beckham, soccer's golden boy, was set to grace the stage of "The Ellen DeGeneres Show."

When Beckham finally stepped onto the set, a torrent of applause and cheers swept across the room. He was every bit the picture of sophistication, clad in a suit that seemed to embody his iconic style, his effortless charm emanating like a magnet.

The conversation started with a light yet sincere homage to Beckham's decorated soccer career. Their banter flowed freely, punctuated with laughter and heartwarming tales from their respective lives. It created a dynamic exchange that pulsed with chemistry.

As the conversation steered into the waters of David Beckham's present ventures, he wore his heart on his sleeve, showing a passion for the beautiful game. His words encapsulated his philanthropic pursuits, spotlighting the power of kindness and the necessity of giving back to the community. The sincerity in his words tugged at the heartstrings of the audience and Ellen.

Beckham, a doting husband and father, vividly depicted his affection for Victoria and their brood. His eyes gleamed with admiration and love as he recounted cherished moments. It was a beautiful intersection of their two lives.

A shift in the narrative then led them to the fashion world and Beckham's reputation as a style icon. With her signature twinkle in her eye, Ellen playfully ribbed him about some of his more memorable hairstyles, sparking laughter that resonated across the studio.

The crescendo of the episode came as a surprise challenge, the brainchild of Ellen's love for unexpected games. A soccer-related test awaited Beckham, who rose to the occasion with his signature grace and finesse.

The studio echoed with cheers as he showcased his extraordinary skill, leaving even the seasoned Ellen in awe of his precision. It was a fitting end to a memorable afternoon.

- **Sherri Shepherd**

The moment Sherri Shepherd stepped onto the Ellen Show, the air crackled with excitement for what was poised to be an unforgettable episode. Sherri, a powerhouse of humor and grace, captivated everyone with her electrifying presence. As she unfolded the narrative of her career, her journey from the early days of stand-up comedy to her celebrated stint on "The View" captivated the audience, showcasing her remarkable resilience through both her successes and challenges.

The conversation then took a deep dive into the significance of representation in the media, a topic Sherri holds dear. She eloquently highlighted the critical need for a variety of stories and voices in television and film, advocating for the importance of showcasing diverse narratives.

Sherri's altruistic spirit glimmered as she spoke about her dedication to uplifting underserved communities. Her call to action, urging viewers to embrace the chance to make a difference, resonated deeply.

As the episode neared its end, Sherri's heartfelt thanks for the opportunity to share her story on such a renowned platform was moving. She lauded Ellen for her indelible impact on the entertainment world and her unwavering commitment to kindness. Their heartfelt farewells wrapped up the episode beautifully, leaving viewers inspired and touched by the warmth and wisdom shared on stage.

- **Joe Biden**

The day Joe Biden, the 46th President of the United States, graced "The Ellen DeGeneres Show" was truly one for the books. Ellen greeted him with heartfelt congratulations on his inauguration, setting the stage for a memorable conversation. Together, they navigated a blend of policy discussions and light-hearted exchanges, showcasing the President's down-to-earth demeanor and quick wit.

Amidst the policy talk, their banter kept the atmosphere vibrant, highlighting the President's approachable side. Yet, it was their shared reflections on the importance of family that truly resonated, painting a picture of Biden not just as a leader but as a family man deeply committed to his loved ones.

This episode didn't just entertain; it offered a glimpse into President Biden's genuine warmth and lifelong dedication to serving the public. Ellen's platform provided the perfect backdrop to explore the human aspects of political leadership, leaving viewers with a deeper appreciation for the person behind the presidency.

- **Serena Williams**

Tennis champion Serena Williams shared her journey with Ellen, highlighting persistence and advocacy for women's rights and racial equality. A humorous tennis game added levity, showcasing Serena's athleticism and Ellen's comedic flair.

- **Alicia Keys**

Alicia Keys, a talented musician and philanthropist, also made a captivating appearance on Ellen's show. The episode featured laughter, heartfelt moments, and soul-stirring music.

CHAPTER 4
THE COMEDIC CHAMELEON

Ellen DeGeneres is a radiant beacon in this world, her humor slicing through the gloom, turning every dark corner into a warm glow of joy. She pirouettes through life's unpredictable tides with the finesse of a seasoned comedian, her vast comedic arsenal morphing to match the contours of each moment, no matter how shadowed it might be.

Ellen's brand of humor is more than a string of jokes; it's a rich tapestry laced with the shimmering strands of her influence, where every laugh carries a piece of her spirit, her ethos. Her jests echo with a resonance that carries her voice far beyond the confines of a stage. Her comedy acts as both shield and sword, packaging her convictions not in preachy tones but through the sharpness of a punchline, making the sometimes bitter pill of truth not just palatable but enjoyable.

Her brilliant wit shines brightest on the "The Ellen DeGeneres Show set." Within this sanctuary of laughter, Ellen weaves her life experiences into the fabric of the show, each narrative more vibrant and complex than the last. One unforgettable segment features her brandishing a seemingly mundane object—a Bic pen designed for women. To the untrained eye, it appears merely as a pen, but it transforms into a mighty instrument of comedic gold in Ellen's hands.

The audience leans in, hanging on her every word, as Ellen embarks on her monologue, her voice dripping with that distinctive sparkle of mirth.

She starts with a seemingly innocuous remark about women's rights, "Women can vote now, I think since 1983," she jests, a twinkle in her eye. "We can wear pants, drive at night, all these things have happened." The absurdity is palpable, and the satire is sharp. Ellen uses the pen, this ordinary everyday object, as a lance to joust with the absurdities of gender stereotypes, mocking the belated recognition of women's rights.

The laughter that fills the room is not just a reaction to a well-told joke but an acknowledgment of the truth wrapped in humor. Beneath the surface of her comedic performance lies a powerful message, a critique wrapped in velvet, delivered with a smile yet striking at the heart of societal norms. Through her unique blend of humor and insight, Ellen transforms a simple segment into a profound commentary, proving once again that laughter can be the most effective vehicle for change.

- In Ellen's hands, a Bic pen transcends its original purpose to become a vessel of satire, subtly highlighting the struggle for equality, especially in terms of women's rights. With her comedic genius, she wraps profound messages in absurdity, transforming even a simple pen into a powerful tool for social commentary.
- In "Relatable," her stand-up performance, Ellen skillfully navigates between jokes and storytelling, turning mundane activities like dining out and travel mishaps into humorous anecdotes. She boldly shares aspects of her life that many celebrities avoid discussing—how her reality vastly differs from that of her audience.
- Ellen brings her enchanting humor to various platforms, whether it's a talk show or a university commencement speech. She has the unique ability to draw laughter from the most stoic audiences, lighten hearts, and open minds, making her messages resonate more deeply.
- At a particular university event, Ellen captivated the students with her distinct comedic approach, engaging them with her humor. She humorously remarked, "I assumed you'd all be alumni—well-known, successful past students. But I see some of you still need to

graduate. I should mention I didn't attend university here, and I don't know if President Cowan is aware that I didn't attend any university at all. I'm not saying you wasted time or money, but look at me—I'm a massive celebrity." Her playful wording and light-hearted take on the value of college education set a relaxed and engaging tone.

- Her joke about the dubious measure of college success being the ability to consume twenty tequila shots sends the audience into fits of laughter. Ellen's talent for capturing her audience's attention with humor from the outset is an art few possess.
- The "Ellen DeGeneres Show" exemplifies Ellen's ability to blend humor with genuine connection, captivating millions of viewers. Her iconic entrance, dancing through the audience, primes the atmosphere for excitement and laughter. Ellen's surprise gifts to her audience further showcase her generous spirit, making each episode a blend of joy and surprise.
- Ellen has garnered public affection throughout the years, with her star continuously rising. She married Australian actress Portia de Rossi -- best known for the TV show, "Arrested Development" -- on August 16, 2008. This was just months after the California Supreme Court overturned a ban on gay marriage.

Despite media storms and controversy, she remains an indomitable figure, loved by millions for her laughter and authenticity.

Interestingly, Ellen's comedic persona takes on a distinct character on the standup stage compared to her daytime talk show.

"Relatable," her first standup special since 2003's "Here and Now," marked Ellen's much-anticipated return to the comedy circuit at age 60. This was Ellen as audiences had not seen her in years—Ellen, the standup comedian, the one who didn't hand out gifts. Instead, she gave away abundant laughter through observations about holiday expectations, prescription drug commercials, and entertaining exchanges of pet videos with her wife, Portia de Rossi.

A remarkable element of "Relatable" was the honest candor she brought to the stage. She touched on deeply personal topics—losing a former girlfriend that fueled her first standup material and her battle with depression following her public coming out and the cancellation of her sitcom "Ellen" in 1998. In this standup, Ellen even surprises the audience with an occasional expletive, like when she humorously mourns the holes in her favorite socks.

Ellen DeGeneres embarked on a captivating eight-night tour, capturing the essence of her comedic prowess in a standup special. Motivated by her agent's encouragement, Ellen DeGeneres ventured beyond the familiar confines of her daytime talk show. With a new theme focusing on the universal aspects of human experience, her comedy set sought to highlight the threads that bind us together. Ellen excitedly previewed her upcoming Netflix special, offering sneak peeks into her creative endeavors from the serene backdrop of French Polynesia. This adventure beautifully intertwined her comedic legacy with current insights, paying homage to the unifying force of laughter and the shared journey of humanity.

CHAPTER 5

THE WALTZ OF LOVE AND TABOOS IN HOLLYWOOD

Ellen DeGeneres and Anne Heche's love story was nothing short of a Hollywood spectacle. Ellen recalls their first encounter, painting Anne as a comet whose unparalleled charm lit up her world: "She was a burst of light in a realm of beauty, truly one of a kind."

Yet, their romance wasn't without its trials. At the 1997 "Volcano" movie premiere, choosing to debut as a couple sparked significant controversy. Anne faced a tough choice: her career or Ellen. Boldly, she chose love over constraints.

After three vibrant years, their journey together ended on good terms in 2000. Anne's life then intertwined with Coleman Laffoon, but fate took a sorrowful turn with her passing in 2022. Ellen's heartfelt tribute reflected the deep loss felt by many: "Today, the universe mourns. My thoughts are with Anne's loved ones."

Ellen's quest for connection led her to Alexandra Hedison in 2001. However, their paths diverged in 2004, paving the way for Ellen's storied love with Portia de Rossi. Alexandra, too, found happiness with Jodie Foster. Through ups and downs, their stories remind us of love's resilience and the beauty of forging new beginnings.

Ellen DeGeneres's journey intertwines personal battles and public triumphs, showcasing her resilience, bravery, and societal influence. Let's trace the milestones that sculpted her into an emblem of courage and LGBTQ+ advocacy.

In a bold move that marked a personal and professional turning point, Ellen publicly came out in April 1997. This brave act led to the cancellation of her sitcom and a challenging period in her career, casting her into what she described as a "deep depression." Despite facing harsh backlash, this moment fueled her commitment to LGBTQ+ rights, illustrating her resilience and the significant impact of her advocacy.

Ellen's narrative includes confronting personal demons, particularly a harrowing experience from the 1970s she courageously shared in interviews. Following her mother's breast cancer diagnosis, Ellen became a victim of sexual manipulation by her stepfather under the guise of health concerns. These revelations not only highlight her bravery but also contribute meaningfully to the discourse on sexual abuse, illuminating the complexities of her journey.

Her love story with Portia de Rossi, which began in 2004, has captivated the public eye. Transitioning from previous relationships, they navigated initial hurdles, including Portia's struggle with her sexuality and their personal commitments. Yet, their undeniable bond blossomed, becoming a testament to their love and resilience.

Ellen shared in a 2005 PEOPLE interview, "We were each committed to someone else when we first met, but the connection between us was undeniable. Facing it was a challenge." Their love story culminated in marriage in 2008, a union celebrated and admired by many.

Portia has publicly expressed her admiration for Ellen, highlighting her positive influence. In a 2009 interview with Oprah Winfrey, Portia disclosed, "I was immediately attracted to Ellen, but being in the closet and concerned about my career made the thought of being associated with the world's most famous lesbian overwhelming." Despite these fears, their relationship flourished, showcasing a powerful example of love overcoming societal pressures and personal fears.

Ellen DeGeneres's story is a testament to vulnerability, courage, and authenticity. Facing backlash for coming out, sharing her abuse experiences, and celebrating her love with Portia de Rossi, Ellen's journey showcases resilience and a commitment to truth. These experiences shaped her into a symbol of LGBTQ+ advocacy, emphasizing kindness, generosity, and equality.

During challenging times, Ellen relied on therapy and antidepressants, facing a stalled career and overwhelming public scrutiny. "The anger I felt was visceral," she revealed. Her struggles underscore her strength and determination to stand in her truth, using her platform to challenge societal norms and inspire authenticity.

Ellen's impact goes beyond her personal story, serving as a catalyst for change and hope. Through laughter, generosity, and a pursuit of equality, she fosters a more inclusive world, demonstrating that love, authenticity, and resilience can make a difference.

Ellen, who married Portia in a symbolic ceremony in 2008, has since reconciled with the criticism and backlash she faced after coming out. She reflected, "I understand it now. I disrupted the status quo. Despite sitcoms frequently showcasing intimacy and sex, my show was labeled 'Adult Content.' That felt like a slap in the face. Yet now, I notice regret in the eyes of those who once ostracized me."

During an appearance on Dax Shepard's "Armchair Expert" podcast, Ellen opened up about the emotional toll of becoming fodder for late-night comedy shows and feeling alienated from Hollywood. "I felt constantly mocked. It was excruciatingly painful."

Despite the arduous journey, Ellen took intentional steps towards self-reconstruction. She turned to meditation, sought comfort in writing, and took up physical exercise. By dedicating herself to her recovery, she overcame her depression. Today, she stands as a towering figure in television, epitomizing resilience and victory.

CHAPTER 6
A RAINBOW REVOLUTION

Ellen DeGeneres' story is a vibrant tapestry woven with threads of bravery, societal shifts, and a touch of humor. Imagine it's 1994, and Ellen is the star of her own sitcom, "Ellen." Here, she navigates the choppy waters of being a young, single woman, all while hiding her sexuality. Picture the backdrop: a world where the Supreme Court shrugs at discrimination, the shadow of the AIDS epidemic looms, and the gay rights movement is just finding its feet. For many in the LGBTQ+ community, the thought of coming out was a distant dream.

Fast forward to 1996, and the plot thickens with the Defense of Marriage Act (DOMA), a stark reminder of the times' heteronormative grip. Ellen, still in the closet, plays the lead in "Mr. Wrong," searching for love in all the traditionally "right" places, further highlighting the era's expectations.

Then comes 1997, a year that would forever change the channel. Ellen turns her personal truth into a groundbreaking TV moment, bravely coming out on her sitcom. Despite facing a storm of backlash and losing sponsors, this was more than a personal revelation; it was a revolution. Her courage sparked conversations, challenging the status quo and paving the way for acceptance and understanding. Ellen's journey from hiding to headline-making wasn't just about her—it was a beacon of hope and change for many.

Fast forward to the revolutionary year of 2008, during a brief period when same-sex unions were legalized in California, Ellen DeGeneres and Portia de Rossi seized the moment to marry, becoming a beacon of change. Their wedding images, showcasing the couple in radiant white, holding hands, broke through the monotony of heteronormative imagery, symbolizing a modern-day fairytale. This moment was a cultural shift, a landmark in the movement toward equality, as media sage Dietram Scheufele suggested.

Ellen DeGeneres, with her boundless wit and magnetic personality, has become more than just a comedian; she's a force of change, gently nudging society to embrace love in all its forms. Despite the hurdles, Ellen's unwavering positivity and knack for tackling tough issues with humor and grace have nurtured a culture of acceptance and resilience. She's not just making us laugh; she's shaping our values, turning challenges into opportunities for growth, and proving the power of staying true to oneself. Her journey has inspired legions, shining a light on our collective progress and the work still ahead.

Ellen's conversations about homosexuality don't just touch hearts; they move mountains, advocating for a world where respect and equality aren't just ideals but realities. Her joy at the repeal of California's gay marriage ban isn't just personal; it's a victory lap for everyone who values equality. Beyond her show, Ellen has become pivotal in shifting how society views same-sex love.

Ellen and her wife, Portia de Rossi, have been Hollywood staples, gracing red carpets together and living their love story in the public eye. Ellen's courageous coming-out on her sitcom wasn't just a milestone for her but a beacon for change, making her and Anne Heche one of America's most iconic lesbian couples.

Ellen's legacy is not just in laughs but in our strides toward a more inclusive world.

After their separation, Ellen found love with Portia, and they celebrated their union on The Oprah Show, expressing gratitude and a sense of belonging. They also shared their disappointment over the reversal of Proposition 8. Portia sought to legally change her name, underscoring her commitment. Despite persistent rumors, Ellen dismissed any notion of a split, emphasizing their love and finding humor in the tabloid stories.

Amidst the rumors, Ellen and Portia welcomed a new family member—a puppy named Kid, a playful nod to the frequent question, "When are you and Portia going to have a kid?" With humor and grace, Ellen addressed this on her show, saying, "So, now we have a Kid. That should stop the questions."

Ellen shared her secret to a successful marriage in an interview with PEOPLE, highlighting the importance of prioritizing each other, even above their careers and maintaining a sense of gratitude. "We remind each other constantly how lucky we are," she said. "Sometimes it's lying in bed at night before I go to sleep, and I just say thank you to whatever or whoever is out there. I've gotten to a point where I really am just settled. Really. I know that I'm not going anywhere. She's not going anywhere."

On Ellen's 60th birthday, Portia surprised her with two deeply significant gifts: a gorilla sanctuary named after DeGeneres in a Rwandan national park and the Ellen DeGeneres Wildlife Fund.

The Wildlife Fund was aimed at preserving and protecting endangered animals and wildlife, while the sanctuary would serve as a permanent and safe home for the Dian Fossey Gorilla Fund.

"For your 60th birthday, this gift had to be really special and represent who you are and what you care about," Portia said on Ellen's talk show. "What you care about is—what you were influenced by and what has made you the amazing person that you are today."

In 2018, Ellen and Portia celebrated their tenth wedding anniversary by sharing images and videos from their private ceremony. They also spoke about philosopher Wayne Dyer's speech at their wedding, emphasizing the importance of marriage equality.

In a 2016 speech, former President Barack Obama recognized the significance of Ellen's 1997 coming-out moment and its broad societal impact. He commented on the courage it took for Ellen, an individual loved by many, to challenge societal assumptions and push for acceptance.

This era also marked a shift in TV portrayals of LGBTQ+ characters. Shows like "Will & Grace," "Queer as Folk," and "The L Word" brought stories of gay and lesbian characters into mainstream entertainment. Eventually, it became less noteworthy for a TV character to identify as gay. The 2016/17 GLAAD report celebrated the highest number of LGBTQ+ characters in TV history.

Now, TV shows regularly feature LGBTQ+ plotlines, with shows like "American Horror Story," "Grey's Anatomy," "Empire," "Game of Thrones," "Modern Family," and "Pretty Little Liars," incorporating queer characters into their narratives.

However, despite these strides, there is still a lack of gay lead characters in mainstream media, signaling that progress in representation is an ongoing journey.

Ellen DeGeneres and Portia de Rossi's love story isn't just their own; it mirrors a broader narrative of societal change and the ongoing fight for LGBTQ+ visibility and equality. As they step out together, their union shines a light on both personal and collective journeys toward acceptance. Even as television slowly warms up to the idea of gay leads, skepticism lingers. Yet, hope blooms in the world of streaming platforms, where queer characters can step beyond stereotypes and be seen for their full humanity. This leap forward in representation is more than just entertainment—it's a lifeline of validation for the LGBTQ+ community and a bridge of empathy for those outside it.

The tale of Ellen and Portia is more than a love story; it's a chapter in the larger saga of progress, reflecting the strides we've made and the distance we've yet to cover. Their visibility not only celebrates love in its myriad forms but also underscores the importance of continuing to push boundaries, fostering a world where everyone can see themselves reflected on the screen and in society at large. Their journey, marked by love, resilience, and laughter, offers a beacon of hope, reminding us that while the path toward acceptance and understanding is long, it's one we're navigating together.

CHAPTER 7
THE UNFURLING OF AN ENCHANTING EMPIRE

Ellen DeGeneres, a sparkling jewel in the crown of entertainment, made her grand entrance with the hit sitcom "Ellen" on March 29, 1994. But that was just the warm-up. As the 21st century dawned, Ellen didn't just walk into the movie scene; she dove in headfirst. Voicing Dory in "Finding Nemo" (2003), she helped the film swim its way to an astounding $871 million globally, making it the second highest-grossing film of the year.

Yet, Ellen's dazzle extends beyond the big screen. With her infectious laughter and dance moves that could get a statue grooving, she's also a mastermind in advertising and a superhero in philanthropy. Imagine this: It's November 2004, and Ellen pops up on your TV in an American Express ad, winning over hearts with her undeniable charm. Leap to 2006, and there she is in a stunning black-and-white ad with a crew of animals crafted by Ogilvy & Mather, which clinched the Emmy for Outstanding Commercial in 2007. Legendary, isn't it?

And then, Ellen did something groundbreaking. On February 25, 2007, she hosted the Academy Awards, marking a milestone as the first openly gay person to take on the role. With her signature inclusivity and humor, she didn't just host the Oscars; she owned them, earning rave reviews and an Emmy nod for her standout performance. Ellen's not just a star; she's a trailblazer, making waves with her every move.

In September 2008, Ellen DeGeneres didn't just tiptoe into the beauty realm; she stormed in, joining forces with CoverGirl Cosmetics in a move that set tongues wagging. Eyebrows lifted at her alliance with Procter & Gamble, a company not without its animal testing controversies. Yet by January 2009, Ellen was all aglow as the radiant face of CoverGirl, dazzlingly branching into beauty campaigns.

But Ellen's ambition to ignite transformation truly shone in December 2011 at the "Change Begins Within" gala by the David Lynch Foundation. Far from your typical gala, this event was a dynamic crusade for inner peace and wellness, showcasing Ellen's capacity to influence far beyond the glitter of showbiz.

2012 ushered in Ellen as the new face of J.C. Penney, a collaboration that underscored her universal charm and ability to resonate with a broad audience. This magic touch not only bolstered her influence but also lined her pockets with a cool $53 million that year, per Forbes. Ellen DeGeneres: more than just a celebrity, she's a catalyst for change and a wizard at creating ripples, no matter the field.

October 2014 marked the launch of her E.D. on Air line on QVC, introducing a range of home products that reflected her personal style.

Returning to host the Oscars in 2014, DeGeneres facilitated a moment that turned into social media gold: a star-studded selfie aiming to break the record for most retweets. Joined by Meryl Streep and a host of celebrities, the photo quickly surpassed the previous record held by Barack Obama. With over 3.4 million retweets as of May 2017, this selfie became an iconic Oscars moment, spawning parodies and cementing DeGeneres's impact on both television and social media history.

In 2018, Ellen extended her collaboration with TCL as the Official TV of The Ellen DeGeneres Show and launched EV1 with Walmart on September 10, offering affordable fashion options.

Through these ventures, Ellen has demonstrated her ability to inspire and enact positive change, cementing her status as a beloved public figure and advocate for inclusivity.

Striving for diversity, Ellen plunged into the world of reality television a few months later. Taking over the reins from Paula Abdul, she graced the judging panel of "American Idol." However, despite a five-year contract worth a fortune, she left after a single season, citing the experience as a mismatch.

Ellen's departure from "American Idol" was made easier by her more lucrative gig hosting "The Ellen DeGeneres Show," where she reportedly raked in an eye-watering $50 million per season.

In 2010, she expanded her empire into the realm of melody. Ellen founded her record label, eleven eleven. She began signing a tantalizing mix of under-the-radar artists and promising YouTube stars, including Charlie Puth, Greyson Chance, and Jessica Simpson, who released a festive album under the new label.

In the sizzling summer of 2015, Ellen DeGeneres didn't just dip her toes but dove headfirst into the fashion and lifestyle world with the launch of her ED Ellen DeGeneres line. Imagine a collection brimming with Ellen's signature style and infectious charm, spanning everything from chic apparel to must-have accessories and cozy home décor. This bold move didn't just add to her empire—it skyrocketed her net worth to a jaw-dropping $285 million.

But Ellen's talents stretch far beyond the screen and design studio. She's a wordsmith with four books to her credit, weaving her wit and wisdom into pages that fans can't get enough of. Add to this her lifestyle brand, and you've got a recipe for unstoppable success.

Awards? Ellen's got them by the boatload. From the Mark Twain Prize for American Humor to an astonishing 20 PEOPLE'S CHOICE

Awards and the revered Presidential Medal of Freedom in 2016, her trophy shelf is as varied as her talents. And let's not forget January 2020, when Ellen made history yet again by receiving the Carol Burnett Award at the Golden Globes, stepping into the spotlight as the award's first honoree after its legendary namesake.

Ellen DeGeneres: a trailblazer, a trendsetter, and a true icon whose Midas touch and heartfelt humor continue to leave an indelible mark on the world.

In the same season, Ellen ventured into television production, launching the enthralling "Ellen's Design Challenge" on HGTV. Aspiring furniture artisans were set to the task, molding raw materials into extraordinary masterpieces within a single day.

Meanwhile, Ellen's passion for design spilled into the literary world when she published her book, "Home." This elegant hardcover journeyed through many properties that Ellen and her beloved wife, Portia de Rossi, had breathed life into, showcasing their shared passion for renovation and design.

Ever proving her touch to be as golden as the Midas tale, Ellen re-emerged on the big screen in 2016, lending her voice again to the endearing Dory in the sequel, "Finding Dory." The film's success was as vast as the ocean, joining the elusive billion-dollar club and securing its place as the third highest-grossing film of that year.

Striding boldly into the digital age, Ellen established Ellen Digital Ventures, overseeing her highly successful streaming platform, EllenTube. This expansion further bolstered her remarkable fortune, which had swelled to an impressive $360 million by then.

In 2017, Ellen added another feather to her cap as she created and hosted the whimsical "Ellen's Game of Games" on NBC. The show's instant popularity secured its renewal for a third season, reinforcing her influential reign in the television kingdom.

In real estate, Ellen's touch transformed properties into golden assets. With a string of multimillion-dollar homes flipped for a considerable profit, she and Portia reaped a handsome $19 million profit from a Beverly Hills home in 2018—a property they'd held for less than three years.

The year 2018 saw Ellen's entrepreneurial spirit weave a multitude of lucrative partnerships. She extended her deal with the Chinese electronics giant TCL, securing its television sets as the official screens of "The Ellen DeGeneres Show." She also teamed up with Walmart to debut an affordable fashion line, EV1, further diversifying her business portfolio.

Revisiting her roots in comedy after a 15-year intermission, Ellen delivered a Netflix special, "Ellen DeGeneres: Relatable." This triumphant return added a further $20 million to her net worth, propelling it to an astronomical $450 million.

The chronicles of Ellen DeGeneres echo a tale of relentless ambition, proving that with passion and persistence, the stars are within our reach.

ED Ellen DeGeneres, Ellen's lifestyle brand, has soared to success on the wings of her star power and commitment to ethical and sustainable practices.

The brand, imbued with Ellen's spirit and ideals, has stitched fruitful collaborations with retail powerhouses such as Nordstrom and Bed Bath & Beyond. However, what sets the brand apart is its unwavering focus on sustainable materials and ethical manufacturing practices, carving out a niche that harmonizes fashion with responsibility.

The brand's alignment with charitable organizations, including The Ellen Fund, shows a steadfast commitment to global conservation efforts, shedding light on Ellen's dedication to bettering our planet.

Successful partnerships with companies such as Walmart, Wayfair, PetSmart, and Bed Bath & Beyond have yielded commercial success and created spaces that resonate with Ellen's core values of design, positivity, and inclusion. Her range of products, from women's apparel to pet accessories and home décor, now find their home across stores and websites nationwide, enabling a wider audience to share in her vision.

Away from the limelight of commercial success, Ellen's philanthropic spirit stands as a shining beacon. Her unwavering support for many charities and organizations has earned her many accolades, testifying to her generous contributions toward humanity, animals, and the environment.

Ellen's philanthropic endeavors are diverse and profound. She has generously donated millions to battle hunger, fight cancer, and eradicate bullying.

Her active involvement in charitable campaigns such as the Small Change Campaign, Ellen for the Cure Campaign, The Gentle Barn, The Ellen Fund, and the #BeKindtoElephants Campaign further cements her status as a benevolent humanitarian.

Ellen's compassionate heart is also in rhythm with the animal kingdom, which is clear in initiatives such as the Adopt-a-Turkey program, which encourages a more compassionate approach to Thanksgiving traditions.

The Ellen DeGeneres Wildlife Fund, an arm of the Digit Fund, even extends its benevolence to the conservation of gorillas by selling themed footwear and T-shirts.

In the sphere of education, Ellen's generosity illuminates the path. Aside from offering substantial financial aid, she uses her comedic prowess to highlight the importance of education, reinforcing her mission to effect positive change in the world.

One memorable manifestation of this mission happened under the Louisiana sun in 2006. At Tulane University's commencement ceremony, after the speeches of political heavyweights Bill Clinton and George H. W. Bush, the audience welcomed an unexpected figure: Ellen DeGeneres. Clad in a bathrobe and slippers, her humor shone brightly, adding to the day's warmth. Ellen's unique charm and dedication to making the world a better place were on full display that day.

Ultimately, Ellen's fame is a testament to her talent and a reflection of her generosity. Having reached the pinnacle of entertainment, she didn't pause but continued to scale new heights, transforming her fame into a conduit for positive change.

Her philanthropy and commercial success are interwoven, each amplifying the other, revealing the multifaceted gem that is Ellen DeGeneres.

Ellen is also an active philanthropist, donating to causes such as hunger relief, cancer research, and animal welfare. Her charitable initiatives include the Small Change Campaign, Ellen for the Cure Campaign, The Gentle Barn, The Ellen Fund, and the #BeKindtoElephants Campaign.

One of her most notable philanthropic ventures is the Ellen Fund, which supports a science and education campus for wild mountain gorillas in Rwanda. Ellen's imprint is also on her footwear and T-shirts, whose proceeds support gorilla conservation.

Ellen DeGeneres combines humor and generosity to impact education significantly. She demonstrated this commitment at Tulane University's 2006 commencement, where she humorously wore a bathrobe and slippers, lightening the event's tone.

Ellen leverages her entertainment and business success to effect change in various areas, notably education, showcasing that success involves uplifting others. Her actions exemplify using one's platform to promote education and make a meaningful difference.

CHAPTER 8
A DANCE OF BENEVOLENCE AND LAUGHTER

Ellen DeGeneres, a beacon of love and generosity, danced through 2022 with a flair that could only be hers. Imagine her as the star performer in life's grandest show, where her every move—a spin, a twirl—casts spells of charity. On her renowned show and at dazzling award nights, Ellen didn't just wear clothes; she wore stories, each sparkling with laughter and goodwill. These weren't just garments; they were tickets to a charity gala, auctioned not for applause but to shine a light on causes close to her heart.

Ellen didn't stop there. She turned her spotlight onto society's shadows, launching the "Be Kind" campaign with a heart-rending Public Service Announcement. Teaming up with The Trevor Project and the Pacer Center, she didn't just speak; she shared a piece of her soul. This wasn't your everyday PSA. It was Ellen, raw and real, tackling bullying head-on. Her plea wasn't just heard; it was felt, a rallying cry against the darkness, urging us all to fight the good fight against bullying with compassion and understanding.

Humor wasn't merely Ellen's talent but a magical wand she waved, transforming sorrow into laughter. Amid the turmoil in her early life, she turned to humor, conjuring joy amidst despair: "Post the shattering of her family unit at 13, she and her mother, Betty, who is one of her strongest supporters and an active member of PFLAG (Parents, Friends, and Family of Lesbians and Gays), migrated like phoenixes to Texas.

During this period of upheaval, DeGeneres unfurled the charm of laughter to lift her mother's drooping spirits" (Ellen DeGeneres, St. James Encyclopedia). Ellen danced in the face of adversity, coaxing smiles where there were none, her buoyant optimism serving as a beacon for her mother in stormy times.

Optimism was her shield, her aegis against life's relentless blows: "Caught off-guard at a public event once, DeGeneres ingeniously wove her surprise into a tapestry of humor, captivating her audience. Her nimble wit unfurled a cascade of requests for her to grace the stages with her stand-up comedy" (Ellen DeGeneres, Newsmakers). Ellen transformed each pitfall into a playful pirouette, using her humor to illuminate the lives of others.

Ellen's luminescent optimism pairs exquisitely with her daring outspokenness, creating an irresistible cadence, particularly resonant when championing gay marriage and rights. A proud member of the LGBTQ+ community, DeGeneres bravely donned her armor and became a beacon of advocacy, fearlessly leading the charge by premiering an eye-opening coming-out episode on her sitcom Ellen: The show became a battleground of opinions when DeGeneres acknowledged her homosexuality, introducing episodes with gay narratives, which invited criticism" (Roll Over, Ward Cleaver).

Despite facing dissension and turbulence, Ellen DeGeneres' courageous stance was a testament to her pride in her identity. An ABC affiliate in Birmingham, Alabama, refused to air the landmark episode, and fearing controversy, some of the show's sponsors, including Daimler Chrysler, withdrew their advertisements.

DeGeneres marched forward, her head held high, her "coming out" a flag she bore with unshakable pride.

Despite the tumult that shadowed her personal revelation, her decision ultimately emerged victorious, becoming a lighthouse for other characters of the same identity: "DeGeneres carved a path in the rugged terrain of television for other openly gay and lesbian characters" (Roll Over, Ward Cleaver). Grasping her influential power as a TV icon, DeGeneres weaved a transformative impact on society's perception of the LGBTQ+ community. She became a stalwart figure, someone to admire and aspire toward, a beacon of courage for every person grappling with their identity.

Ellen thrives in her unique rhythm, unafraid to sway to her music in a crowd marching to a different beat. Whether she's crafting jokes to spark joy or expending effort in humanitarian pursuits, she remains committed to her authentic self. Her anthem of kindness resonates: "Be kind, amicable, and respectful, even if you encounter unkindness. Rise above their level." These pearls of wisdom from Ellen serve as a guiding light, inspiring one to be the greater person in any situation. Ellen's relentless pursuit of a better world makes her a role model; her confidence in facing challenges inspires hope for making impactful changes, such as advocating for equal treatment of the gay community or striving for global peace.

Ellen DeGeneres is more than a prism refracting laughter; she is a valiant knight, a selfless philanthropist, and a trailblazer carving paths through societal norms. Despite facing personal struggles with self-image, her authenticity, the vibrancy of her spirit, and her unwavering strength inspire one to mirror the same courage and optimism in one's life. When in need of a surge of confidence or a hearty laugh, turning toward the lively figure dancing on the soundstage, the radiant Ellen DeGeneres can fill the heart with hope and inspiration.

For those who dare to look closer beyond her comedic exterior will find a powerful activist, a beacon of generosity, and the architect of a thousand smiles.

In her childhood musings, Ellen DeGeneres never imagined she'd become a vanguard in the battle for LGBTQ+ equality. Yet, in 1997, she boldly tore down the encased closet she'd been tucked into since her early days as a standup comedian.

Much like the audacious pioneers before her, Ellen braved the treacherous frontier, cognizant of the potential pitfalls awaiting her journey. She risked losing everything she'd painstakingly built, including her wildly successful sitcom featuring her character, Ellen Morgan.

As Ellen and her on-screen persona collectively stepped into the light, the ensuing disruption was of epic proportions. The backlash comprised an onslaught of hate mail, death threats, and, ultimately, the cancellation of her cherished show. By the time of her Making Gay History interview in 2001, Ellen's future was uncertain. Little did anyone predict the meteoric rise her star would witness and that she'd garner accolades as prestigious as the Presidential Medal of Freedom.

A decade after the iconic episode, Laura Dern (a guest star playing Ellen Morgan's love interest) reflected on the repercussions of her participation. In 2017, during the 20th anniversary of Ellen's "coming out" episode, she shared her experiences with her talk show audience. She acknowledged, "I am proud of that. I'm thankful."

Before Ellen's courageous admission, LGBTQ+ representation in entertainment was mostly limited to the 'celluloid closet.' The HIV/AIDS pandemic that swept the globe in the 1980s and 90s cast a deathly shadow over the LGBTQ+ community. It was a turbulent period marked by federal legislation like the Defense of Marriage Act

(DOMA) and "Don't Ask, Don't Tell," signaling that discrimination against LGBTQ+ individuals was legally permissible.

Understanding the societal context that framed Ellen's coming out magnifies its significance. Ellen's narrative successfully humanized the gay community, accentuating the language of equality and sameness. As former President Obama poignantly noted, "She could be our neighbor, colleague, or sister."

The importance of this "sameness" surfaced during the politically charged times of 2003 when then-President George W. Bush declared Iraq the "central front" in the "war on terror." Ellen intended to dispel divisive notions, showing that gay individuals — devout and patriotic Americans, much like her — were a part of the collective 'us.'

Likeness fosters likability. Ellen masterfully encapsulated this with her "Be Kind" motto and her character's embodiment of this ethos.

The quintessential lesbian on mainstream television was a balancing act: not too feminine or masculine. Ellen exuded an affable androgyny with the right hint of lipstick, which welcomed her into millions of American homes.

However, as time revealed, this pursuit of relatability—tied to ratings—entrapped Ellen. She found herself bound by the constraints of likability, unable to show human imperfections. She often acknowledged the constricting influence of her "Be Kind" motto.

The socio-cultural landscape has evolved since the premiere of "The Ellen DeGeneres Show." Visibility for marginalized communities is no longer the sole pathway to acceptance. People who occupy privileged positions, such as Ellen, are responsible for addressing social problems, transcending the performative symbolism of acceptance, and challenging the very systems that perpetuate inequality.

Ellen DeGeneres, a spokesperson for LGBT visibility, is at a cultural crossroads. Once seen as the face of wholesome respectability, a bridge between worlds, whispering to mainstream America, "We're just like you," she now finds herself at odds with a shifting landscape. As Keating notes, this "respectability" has lost favor among the more radical factions of the LGBT community, who seek not assimilation but liberation.

Heather Hogan of Auto Straddle observes that the call for civility often mutes the marginalized, stressing that kindness is not justice. "Being nice isn't enough," she pens with a forceful ink, emphasizing that the fight isn't about "getting along" but rather about the fundamental human rights of those oppressed, bearing the brunt of systemic violence born of white supremacy.

Our societal tapestry has shifted toward authenticity and accountability, away from the complacent "everything's fine" narrative. Yet, Ellen, a trailblazer in one revolution, seems to have stalled in the face of this one.

Her behavior in the backstage alleys of her show has raised questions, painting a picture that contrasts sharply with her kindness-first philosophy.

In a revealing chat with The Hollywood Reporter, Ellen DeGeneres shrugged off accusations of a toxic workplace as "stupid," positioning herself more as a victim than someone willing to take accountability. Interestingly, she mentioned a lack of platform as her reason for not addressing the concerns despite having a massive online presence, including EllenTube, at her disposal.

Ellen claimed her mission was always about spreading kindness and tolerance. Yet, she hesitated to own up to the actions that led to the controversy. She lamented the pleasure some find in negativity without acknowledging how her own lack of action may have fed into the toxic atmosphere.

Announcing her exit from the show after 19 seasons because "it's just not a challenge anymore," Ellen stands at a crossroads. She has a golden opportunity to embrace accountability, reflect, evolve, and take responsibility. Once hailed as a beacon of courage, she now teeters on the edge of being labeled a hypocrite. Yet, there's still hope for her to rewrite her narrative. Her legacy isn't set in stone; a path to redemption is still possible.

Ellen DeGeneres's impact on American culture cannot be understated. A trailblazing LGBTQ+ figure, she has hit several significant milestones:

Coming Out: In 1997, on her hit T.V. sitcom, "Ellen," she came out as gay, becoming one of the first openly gay public figures in Hollywood. This courageous act thrust LGBTQ+ issues into the mainstream.

Emmy Award Wins: Ellen has clinched many Emmy Awards throughout her career, including multiple wins for her daytime talk show, "The Ellen DeGeneres Show," one of the most successful talk show hosts in history, her show has been a fixture since 2003.

Ellen's legacy is a mixed tapestry of courage, kindness, controversy, and alleged hypocrisy. As the final act unfolds, she stands at a crossroads, her next steps likely to define how she is remembered.

Ellen DeGeneres's comedic roots run deep, having cut her teeth as a standup comedian in the 80s and 90s. Her humor, a relatable tapestry of everyday experiences and observations, resonated widely, earning her a reputation as a witty and insightful humorist.

Her comedy painted the mundane in brilliant strokes, leaving audiences doubled over in laughter, caught in the charm of her comedic craft.

Her influence extends beyond the stage, shaping our society through philanthropy.

Ellen DeGeneres, known for her humor and deep compassion for animals, has been a vocal advocate for veganism and animal rights. Ellen and her wife, Portia de Rossi, both embraced a vegan lifestyle, showcasing their commitment to animal welfare. Ellen took her passion a step further by launching "Going Vegan with Ellen," a website dedicated to vegan outreach, sharing tips and recipes, and encouraging the adoption of a plant-based lifestyle. Although her ambitious plan to open a vegan tapas bar in Bokado, in Los Angeles, didn't materialize, her dedication to promoting veganism didn't wane. Her talk show website even featured a section titled "Going Vegan with Ellen," where she championed "Meatless Mondays" and shared vegan recipes to inspire her audience.

However, in a turn of events, Ellen revealed in 2016 that she had reintroduced fish into her diet and confirmed during her 2018 stand-up comedy special, Relatable, that she had moved away from a strictly vegan lifestyle. Despite this change in her diet, Ellen's commitment to animal welfare remains unwavering.

Ellen has actively used her platform to support animal protection efforts. She has repeatedly invited Wayne Pacelle, the Humane Society of the United States CEO, to discuss animal protection legislation on her show. Her efforts were recognized in 2009 when PETA named her their "Woman of the Year." In 2013, she generously donated $25,000 to oppose Ag-Gag legislation in Tennessee, aiming to protect the rights of undercover investigators to expose animal abuse on farms. Moreover, Ellen served as a campaign ambassador for Farm Sanctuary's Adopt-A-Turkey Project in 2010, urging her audience to adopt a turkey for Thanksgiving instead of eating one, promoting kindness and a shift in traditional holiday practices towards more compassionate choices.

Ellen's influence on American culture, particularly for the LGBTQ+ community, has been profound. She defied stereotypes, dismantled barriers, and laid a path for future LGBTQ+ artists in the entertainment industry. Her open-hearted courage offered representation and hope to many, asserting that one's identity should never be a hurdle to success.

But it isn't just the grand gestures. Ellen's kind heart echoes in her everyday actions. Through her show, she contacts individuals seeking help, lending her support to uplift their cause. Her genuine engagement and generosity make her show more than entertainment - it's a beacon of hope for many.

Perhaps one of the most enduring legacies of her show is the creative games she hosts, inviting audience participation. They might seem fun, but there's often an undercurrent of purpose, whether raising money or awareness.

The games, woven into the show's fabric, serve as a platform for charity, her challenges often tied to donations. The more the audience accomplishes, the more she donates.

Philanthropy is integral to Ellen's life, as shown by her commitment to various causes. She joined forces with Ben Affleck to launch the Small Change Campaign to battle hunger across the United States. Her altruism extends to fighting cancer, ending bullying, and many other noble causes.

Ellen DeGeneres is more than a comedian; she's a societal influencer, philanthropist, and advocate. Her life and career paint a portrait of a woman who never shied away from challenges and always infused her work with purpose, whether through humor, generosity, or advocacy.

As the curtains draw on her show, her impact, both seen and unseen, will continue to resonate.

Ellen DeGeneres's philanthropic reach spans a myriad of causes, each illuminating a different facet of her compassion and commitment to making a difference. Here are some charities she supports:

ACLU of Southern California: Ellen supports the fight for equality and justice, furthered by this influential non-profit organization.

American Wild Horse Preservation Campaign: Her love for animals shines through her contributions to this group that seeks to protect and preserve America's wild horses.

Andre Agassi Foundation for Education: Her commitment to education is highlighted by her support for this foundation that focuses on transforming U.S. public education.

Artists Against Racism: Standing against discrimination, Ellen backs this organization that uses the power of art to fight racism.

Best Friends Animal Society: This organization's mission to make animal shelters in the U.S. no-kill aligns with Ellen's dedication to animal welfare.

Charity: water: Her support for this non-profit helps bring clean and safe drinking water to people in developing countries.

Children's Health Fund: She is dedicated to providing healthcare to America's most disadvantaged children through this organization.

David Lynch Foundation: This foundation's focus on reducing trauma and stress among at-risk populations resonates with Ellen's vision of a healthier society.

Elton John AIDS Foundation: Ellen supports combatting the AIDS epidemic through this international non-profit organization.

Farm Sanctuary: Her love for animals finds another outlet in this organization dedicated to combating the abuses of factory farming.

Feeding America: This U.S. hunger relief organization benefits from Ellen's commitment to fighting against hunger.

GLAAD: As a strong advocate for LGBTQ+ rights, her contributions to this organization help promote acceptance and understanding.

Habitat For Humanity: Her support for this global nonprofit housing organization showcases her belief in the importance of safe and affordable housing.

Heifer International: This charity's mission to end hunger and poverty while caring for the Earth aligns with Ellen's commitment to a healthier world.

Make It Right: This foundation's work in building homes, buildings, and communities for people in need finds an ally in Ellen.

St. Jude Children's Research Hospital: Ellen contributes to the pioneering work of this institution in pediatric treatment and research.

The Trevor Project: Her support for this organization aids in suicide prevention efforts among lesbian, gay, bisexual, transgender, and questioning youth.

Ellen's philanthropy extends her influence far beyond the boundaries of television. Her wide-ranging charitable involvement showcases her as a dynamic agent of change.

Undeterred by industry pressures and public scrutiny, her story is a testament to authenticity's power. As a symbol of hope, courage, and resilience, Ellen DeGeneres remains a bright constellation in the sky of inspirational figures.

CHAPTER 9
THE POWER OF POSITIVITY

Ellen DeGeneres stands as a beacon of hope and positivity, impacting entertainment and beyond. Her kindness philosophy, captured in "Be kind to one another," resonates globally. This section examines Ellen's commitment to positivity and its significant impact on individuals and communities. Through her actions and words, Ellen demonstrates how one person's positivity can inspire a global movement, making the world brighter, one act of kindness at a time.

Ellen's Philosophy on Kindness and Positivity

Ellen's commitment to positivity is equally significant. In a world where negativity often dominates headlines and social media feeds, choosing positivity is revolutionary. Ellen understands the power of positive thinking not only in improving one's own life but also in influencing those around us. Her humor, warmth, and genuine nature are tools she uses to spread this positivity, making it clear that being positive doesn't mean ignoring the realities of the world. Instead, it's about focusing on hope, solutions, and the good in people.

This choice of positivity is also about resilience. Ellen's journey has been filled with challenges and setbacks, from her early career to the backlash she faced after coming out. However, she has consistently chosen to focus on the positive, using her experiences to empathize with others and strengthen her commitment to kindness and positivity.

The Ripple Effect of Kindness and Positivity

The Ripple Effect of Kindness and Positivity is a concept that captures the far-reaching impact our actions can have on the world around us. Originating from the belief that even the smallest act of kindness can set off a chain reaction of positive outcomes, this principle is central to understanding the power behind Ellen DeGeneres's philosophy. Here, we delve deeper into how this ripple effect operates and the transformative potential it holds.

The journey of a thousand ripples begins with a single act. This act can be as simple as a smile, a word of encouragement, or a small deed that shows someone they are seen and valued.

Ellen exemplifies this through her spontaneous acts of generosity on her show, where she not only aids those in immediate need but also inspires her audience to partake in similar acts of kindness. While seemingly small in isolation, each of these actions is the stone thrown into the water, creating the initial splash.

The direct impact of kindness and positivity is the immediate joy, relief, or support experienced by the recipient. However, this impact is not limited to the moment; it often initiates a shift in perspective, encouraging a more optimistic outlook or a renewed belief in the goodness of others. This can mean the difference between despair and hope, isolation and feeling supported for the individual on the receiving end. Ellen's efforts to highlight positive stories and gestures of kindness on her platform offer vivid examples of this impact, showcasing real-life transformations brought about by acts of generosity and compassion.

As waves spread from the point of impact, so too does the influence of an initial act of kindness. Observers, whether directly involved or not, are often moved by the demonstration of compassion and positivity. This inspiration can prompt them to replicate similar gestures in their own lives.

Ellen's reach and visibility magnify this effect, as millions are encouraged to act kindly in their own communities.

The stories shared on her show often lead to viewers undertaking their own initiatives, from fundraising for worthy causes to volunteering their time and resources, thereby extending the chain of positivity further than the original act.

The cumulative effect of these expanding circles of kindness and positivity can lead to broader cultural and societal shifts. When kindness becomes a value that is celebrated and emulated, it fosters an environment where empathy, compassion, and cooperation flourish. Ellen's work, especially her focus on inclusivity and celebrating diversity, contributes to a cultural narrative that values kindness and positivity as societal cornerstones. This can gradually lead to systemic changes, where policies and practices are influenced by a collective commitment to fostering a kinder, more positive world.

Making a Difference: On and Off the Screen

Making a difference on-screen and off has been a hallmark of Ellen DeGeneres's career and personal ethos. Her ability to leverage her platform for the greater good demonstrates the powerful role public figures can play in driving positive change in society. This section explores how Ellen has used her visibility to make a significant impact, detailing both her on-screen initiatives and off-screen philanthropy.

On-Screen Initiatives

Ellen's daytime television show, "The Ellen DeGeneres Show," served as much more than a source of entertainment. It became a powerful vehicle for change, showcasing stories of resilience, kindness, and the human spirit. Through her unique platform, Ellen has:

- Highlighted Unsung Heroes: Ellen frequently invited guests who were making a difference in their communities, thereby shining a spotlight on their efforts and inspiring viewers to take action in their own ways.

- Raised Awareness: Ellen used her show to bring attention to critical social issues, such as bullying, mental health, and LGBTQ+ rights, educating her audience and advocating for change.

- Mobilized Resources for Causes: Whether it was disaster relief, wildlife conservation, or supporting individuals in need, Ellen demonstrated an exceptional ability to mobilize resources, rallying her audience to contribute to various causes.

Ellen's on-screen efforts often extended beyond mere financial assistance; she provided a platform for sharing stories that might otherwise go unheard, fostering a sense of empathy and community among her viewers.

Off-Screen Philanthropy

Beyond the television screen, Ellen's commitment to making a difference is evident in her extensive philanthropic work. Her actions reflect a deep-seated belief in using her resources and influence to support causes close to her heart:

- The Ellen DeGeneres Wildlife Fund: One of Ellen's significant off-screen initiatives is her wildlife fund, which focuses on global conservation efforts, particularly the protection of endangered species. This initiative reflects her passion for animal welfare and environmental conservation.

- Support for Disaster Relief: Ellen has been quick to respond in times of crisis, contributing significant amounts to disaster relief efforts following events like hurricanes, earthquakes, and wildfires. Through monetary donations and fundraising, she has helped provide much-needed assistance to affected communities.

- Advocacy and Charity Work: Ellen's advocacy extends to numerous other causes, including education, children's welfare, and health research. Her support for various charities and non-profits has helped amplify their work and provided them with critical resources.

The Impact of Ellen's Efforts

The impact of Ellen's work, both on and off the screen, is profound. By integrating philanthropy with entertainment, she has created a new paradigm for celebrities engaging with social issues and driving societal progress. Ellen's approach to making a difference has not only provided direct assistance to countless individuals and causes but has also inspired others to act. Her actions encourage a broader culture of generosity and kindness, demonstrating how compassion and a platform can be combined to effect real change.

Stories of Lives Touched

Ellen DeGeneres's philosophy of kindness and positivity is embodied in the transformative experiences of those she has helped. The impact of her generosity extends far beyond the immediate beneficiaries, creating a domino effect of goodwill and inspiring countless others to contribute positively to their communities. By exploring additional stories, we can further appreciate the depth of Ellen's influence and the diverse ways in which her acts of kindness have reverberated through society.

Consider the story of a talented teenager from a low-income family with dreams of becoming a professional artist but facing insurmountable financial barriers to education. Ellen, recognizing the young artist's potential, not only featured his artwork on her show but also provided a scholarship for him to attend a prestigious art school.

Beyond the financial support, the recognition on such a significant platform boosted the teenager's confidence and visibility, opening doors to opportunities that were previously unimaginable. This story highlights how Ellen's support for individuals extends beyond immediate needs, focusing on empowering them to reach their full potential.

Ellen's impact extends to her support for community heroes dedicated to helping others. She assisted a firefighter who was severely injured during a rescue, overwhelmed by medical bills and the threat of losing his home. By providing financial aid and a platform to share his story, she eased his financial burden and highlighted the sacrifices of first responders. This gesture not only changed the firefighter's life but also emphasized the importance of supporting those who risk everything for public safety.

Another poignant example is Ellen's support for a young transgender activist facing bullying and isolation in their community. By inviting the activist to her show, Ellen provided a platform for them to share their story, fostering a broader dialogue around inclusivity, acceptance, and the challenges transgender individuals face. This visibility helped the young activist gain support and resources to continue their advocacy work, illustrating how Ellen's platform can amplify marginalized voices and promote a culture of understanding and empathy.

Ellen's commitment to making a difference extends to global challenges, such as environmental conservation.

Ellen has inspired her audience to become more environmentally conscious and active through her initiatives to protect endangered species and habitats. For example, her campaign to save an endangered animal species not only raised significant funds for conservation efforts but also educated millions about the importance of biodiversity and the threats facing our planet. This story underscores Ellen's role in mobilizing public awareness and action for environmental causes, demonstrating that her influence spans a wide range of societal issues.

CHAPTER 10
THE LEGACY AND LESSONS CARVED BY ELLEN DEGENERES

Ellen DeGeneres didn't just leave a mark on daytime television; she carved an indelible legacy. Her show was a beacon of joy and positivity, a source of inspiration for future hosts, and a powerful platform for marginalized voices. Delving deeper, there are vital life lessons we can glean from Ellen's extraordinary journey:

1) **Embrace your authenticity**: Ellen's choice to come out as gay in 1997 wasn't just an individual decision. It was a trailblazing moment that challenged societal norms and led to a cultural shift toward acceptance and visibility of LGBTQ+ individuals in mainstream media. Ellen's courage to wear her truth on her sleeve despite the backlash and cancellation of her sitcom "Ellen" sparked a wave of change, paving the way for LGBTQ+ individuals in the entertainment industry and beyond.

2) **Radiate positivity**: Ellen DeGeneres' name has become synonymous with positivity, an unshakeable beacon of kindness and optimism. This uplifting philosophy is at the core of her show and has consistently illuminated her entire career.

3) From her early stand-up comedy gigs, where she won audiences over with her exuberant spirit and observational humor, to her television endeavors, where she used humor as a salve, Ellen's unyielding dedication to positivity created an aura of warmth and acceptance.

4) **Use humor as a bonding tool**: Ellen's sparkling humor, dappled with self-deprecation and light-hearted banter, was not merely a tool for entertainment; it was a magical thread that connected her to her guests and viewers. Her knack for infusing humor into ordinary situations and diffusing tense moments brought people together, forging strong bonds and shared laughter.

5) **Pay it forward**: Ellen's generosity is as legendary as her wit. She has consistently leveraged her platform for philanthropy, supporting myriad causes, from animal rights and LGBTQ+ rights to disaster relief efforts. This commitment to giving back has marked Ellen as more than just an entertainer but a true humanitarian.

CONCLUSION

Ellen DeGeneres' journey sparkles as a vibrant lesson in living authentically, radiating positivity, forging deep connections, and giving generously. She's shown us that the sweetest victories are those that lift everyone up. With her luminous advocacy, Ellen shines as a fearless champion for the LGBTQ+ community. Her groundbreaking moment in 1997, where she bravely stepped into her truth as a gay woman, didn't just break barriers; it lit a beacon for LGBTQ+ visibility and carved new avenues for acceptance in the spotlight. Through her foundation, Ellen's ripple of positivity has touched many, especially in supporting lifelines like The Trevor Project, which offers crucial support and hope to LGBTQ+ youth navigating life's storms, aiming to dim the shadows of crisis and prevent suicide with a message of love and acceptance.

Ellen's heart knows no limits. Her generous gifts to the American Red Cross have delivered crucial aid to victims of natural disasters like Hurricanes Katrina and Harvey. This act of kindness is a shining example of how to wield influence for the greater good. Ellen's tireless support highlights the essential role of elevating important voices and the incredible difference one person can make in the lives of many. Her actions remind us that true power lies in giving back and uplifting those in need, transforming adversity into hope and recovery.

Born from adversity, Ellen's spirit gleams like tempered steel. Her tale vividly demonstrates resilience's might, a beacon of human fortitude.

Undaunted by the storm of backlash and criticism after her sitcom character's revelation on "Ellen," she refused to be silenced. Instead, she embraced her first love, stand-up comedy, and in 2003, unfurled her own talk show, "The Ellen DeGeneres Show." This bold move marked a triumphant resurgence, becoming a cultural cornerstone. Yet, in 2020, controversy stirred anew with allegations of toxicity in her workplace. An investigation ensued, leading to the departure of top executives. True to form, Ellen confronted the issue head-on, acknowledging the accusations, extending apologies, and pledging to foster a nurturing, respectful environment.

The story of Ellen DeGeneres exemplifies the indomitable power of resilience. Her relentless determination to overcome adversity shines as a beacon for anyone facing challenges, demonstrating that it's possible to conquer even the most daunting obstacles with grit and tenacity.

Ellen's career is a rich tapestry woven from her passions. Her love for comedy and entertainment ignited a spark that has sustained her impressive career. Her bold move from a successful sitcom to the uncertain world of daytime television reaped huge rewards, cementing her status as an iconic talk show host.

Ellen's journey is marked by a diverse array of experiences, from dominating award shows to exploring film and literature. She has seized every opportunity, constantly reinventing herself and leaving a vibrant mark on the entertainment landscape.

Her influence spans hosting prestigious events like the Oscars, Academy Awards, Grammys, and Primetime Emmys, with her stand-up comedy career taking off in the early 1980s and leading to a notable appearance on "The Tonight Show Starring Johnny Carson" in 1986.

This served as a traditional indicator to both comedians and the entertainment industry that Johnny regarded this individual as exceptionally talented. Ellen was the first female comedian to be invited over, a gesture that signified her unique status.

Ellen DeGeneres has made notable appearances in films such as "Mr. Wrong," "EDtv," and "The Love Letter." She also lent her voice to Dory in Disney/Pixar's "Finding Nemo" and its sequel, "Finding Dory," earning the Saturn Award for Best Supporting Actress for her role in "Finding Nemo."

Ellen DeGeneres made a significant foray into the film industry, showcasing her versatile talent on the silver screen. In "Mr. Wrong" (1996), she embarked on a humorously misguided search for the perfect partner, blending laughter with chaos. Her cinematic journey continued as she starred opposite Matthew McConaughey in the comedy "EDtv" (1999) and took a dramatic turn in "If These Walls Could Talk 2" (2000). In this film, DeGeneres and Sharon Stone shared a love scene that not only made headlines but also demonstrated their compelling chemistry, captivating audiences worldwide.

In 2012, Ellen DeGeneres received the Kennedy Center's Mark Twain Prize for American Humor, recognizing her contribution to comedy. In 2016, she was honored with the Presidential Medal of Freedom for her advocacy and impact.

In 2020, her television legacy was celebrated with the Carol Burnett Award at the Golden Globes, acknowledging her decades of delivering joy and laughter.

In addition to her plethora of accomplishments, Ellen has also contributed her literary prowess to the world, penning down her memoir "Seriously...I'm Kidding" and the whimsical children's book "The Funny Thing Is...." She even lent her distinctive, soothing voice to the narration of Michelle Obama's "Becoming," further highlighting her diverse talents.

Ellen's career is a vibrant kaleidoscope, always embracing new ventures, shifting, and morphing, never stagnant. She hasn't restricted herself to a single stage but danced through various mediums and genres, thus constantly evolving as an artist. Her penchant for exploration has kept her career effervescent and enthralling. It serves as an inspirational beacon for others to leap into the sea of opportunities awaiting them.

A testament to the boundless possibilities that embracing new experiences offers, Ellen is a guiding star for those seeking fulfillment in unexpected arenas.

The warmth of positive influences enveloped Ellen, her wife Portia de Rossi being the beacon that radiates love and support, lighting up her world. She has found a sanctuary in the comforting presence of her family and friends, a nurturing network that holds her aloft.

Despite her dizzying ascent to the pinnacle of success, Ellen has kept her humility, a testament to her grounded nature. Her success has been a whirlwind of applause, yet she has always been anchored in the storm's calm eye, her humility serving as her guiding light. Expressing her gratitude at every juncture, Ellen never loses sight of the blessings that have paved her path.

Ellen's remarkable career has spanned several riveting decades, with each phase unfolding as a captivating narrative in entertainment—from her jovial stand-up comedy to her enchanting presence on her talk show. Amid the glittering success, Ellen remains humble, her gratitude for the opportunities she has embraced steadfast.

Amidst thunderous applause and adoring cheers, Ellen frequently takes a moment to share a heartfelt message, showcasing her gratitude towards her devoted audience. She transforms her platform into a powerhouse of positivity, lending her support to various causes and organizations, epitomizing her steadfast dedication to making a difference.

Guided by her core values, Ellen gracefully navigates the choppy seas of fame. She champions kindness and inclusivity, celebrating the remarkable deeds of unsung heroes and illuminating the world's inherent goodness. Through her actions, Ellen not only entertains but inspires, reminding us all of the power of compassion and connection.

Ellen faces the hurdles and missteps in her career with humility and grace. Instead of responding with defensiveness or retaliation, she takes ownership and works to rectify her mistakes. Her journey stands as a compelling testament to the coexistence of success and humility, showcasing how gratitude and steadfast adherence to personal values provide anchorage in the unpredictable voyage of fame. Ellen DeGeneres embodies the essence of remaining true to oneself, highlighting the significance of staying grounded even in the whirlwind of tremendous success.

45 QUOTES BY ELLEN

1) Be kind to one another.

2) Here are the values that I stand for: honesty, equality, kindness, compassion, treating people the way you want to be treated, and helping those in need. To me, those are traditional values.

3) Find out who you are and be that person. That's what your soul was put on this Earth to be. Find that truth, live that truth, and everything else will come.

4) My grandmother started walking five miles a day when she was sixty. She's ninety-seven now, and we don't know where the hell she is.

5) Trying to get the talk show, looking back on it, we had to beg a lot of station managers to pick up the show because people thought no one would watch it because I'm openly gay.

6) We need more kindness, more compassion, more joy, more laughter. I definitely want to contribute to that.

7) Sometimes, you can't see yourself clearly until you see yourself through the eyes of others.

8) We focus so much on our differences, which is creating, I think, a lot of chaos, negativity, and bullying in the world. And I think everybody should focus on what we all have in common—which is that we all want to be happy.

9) Faith is part of who I am, yes. I was raised as a Christian Scientist. The most important thing I saw every single week on the wall at Sunday school was the Golden Rule.

10) I'd like to be more patient! I just want everything now. I've tried to meditate, but it's really hard for me to stay still. I'd like to try to force myself to do it because everybody says how wonderful meditation is for you, but I can't shut my mind up. So, patience and learning is the key.

11) I work really hard at trying to see the big picture and not getting stuck in my ego. I believe we're all put on this planet for a purpose, and we all have a different purpose... When you connect with that love and that compassion, that's when everything unfolds.

12) I learned compassion from being discriminated against. Everything bad that's ever happened to me has taught me compassion.

13) Right before I decided to come out, I went on a spiritual retreat called 'Changing the Inner Dialogue of Your Subconscious Mind.' I'd never been to anything like it before, and all my friends were taking bets on how long I'd last with no TV, no radio, no phone. But for me, that was the beginning of paying attention to all the little things.

14) The world is full of a lot of fear and a lot of negativity, and a lot of judgment. I just think people need to start shifting into joy and happiness. As corny as it sounds, we need to make a shift.

15) People are constantly asking Portia and me if we are going to have children. We thought about it. We love to be around children after they've been fed and bathed. But we

ultimately decided that we didn't want children of our own. There is far too much glass in our house. 🏳️‍🌈

16) The reason I do what I do is because I was influenced by Steve Martin, Woody Allen, Bob Newhart, Carol Burnett, and Lucille Ball.

17) I was raised around heterosexuals, as all heterosexuals are; that's where we gay people come from... you heterosexuals. 🏳️‍🌈

18) I am saddened by how people treat one another, how we are so shut off from one another, and how we judge one another when the truth is, we are all one connected thing. We are all from the same exact molecules.

19) Even before I knew I was gay, I knew I didn't want to have a child. I knew I didn't want to have one. I never want to have to release it from me. Listen, I love babies. I love children. And I melt when I'm around them. I also love my freedom, and I love that I can sleep at night. 🏳️‍🌈

20) I used to beat myself up about weight and working out, and no matter what I did, I never felt good about myself. I decided to accept myself and know that I am good.

21) When people show me clothing that seems very, very feminine, it's hard for me to embrace that because it just doesn't feel like me. 🏳️‍🌈

22) A lot of money with the wrong career is not going to make you happy. If you have money without happiness, it doesn't mean anything. It's all about happiness.

23) My father was a first reader in the Christian Science Church, which is similar to being a preacher. There was no drinking, smoking, or cursing.

24) Hosting the Oscars is pretty much the scariest thing you can do. To me, this is right up there with bungee jumping!

25) The first house I bought was a little Spanish bungalow on Clinton Street in West Hollywood, right behind the Improv. I was renting it, and I asked the owners if I could buy it; they were really nice and let me work out a deal. And I fixed it up and later sold it. That was when I realized that you can make money if you make some improvements.

26) People give me such a hard time because I don't wear dresses. What's that got to do with anything? 🏳️‍🌈

27) The only thing I really recommend, if you're starting out in stand-up, is not to try to copy anybody else. You can be influenced by people. I was influenced by Steve Martin, Bob Newhart, and Woody Allen, but I never tried to be someone else. I always tried to be myself. And the reason people are successful is they're unique.

28) If we're destroying our trees and destroying our environment and hurting animals and hurting one another and all that stuff, there's got to be a very powerful energy to fight that. I think we need more love in the world.

29) If you're going to be honest with yourself, you have to admit that you go into show business wanting people to talk about you and wanting everyone to know who you are.

30) But that also means there are going to be a whole bunch of people who don't like you. No matter who you are.

31) I'm not an activist; I don't look for controversy. I'm not a political person, but I'm a person with compassion. I care passionately about equal rights. I care about human rights. I care about animal rights.

32) Portia and I constantly say to each other, 'We are so lucky.' Sometimes, it's lying in bed at night before I go to sleep, and I just say thank you to whatever, whoever is out there.

33) I still have the shirt I wore my first time on Johnny Carson's show. Only now, I use it as a tablecloth at dinner parties. It was very blousy.

34) I've been trying to find women writers for my staff for a while now, and I have three women on my staff and three guys, so it's pretty equal. I don't know why that is. It's been the same thing for a while. It's hard for female comedians to stand out. That's weird. That's a shame.

35) Designing is my hobby. If I didn't do what I do for a living—at some point when I don't do this for a living—I'll probably just do design work. I love finding really special pieces of furniture.

36) Usually, I wear tennis shoes because my feet are flat, and it hurts to wear anything other than shoes that are cushiony.

37) I get those fleeting, beautiful moments of inner peace and stillness—and then the other 23 hours and 45 minutes of the day, I'm a human trying to make it through in this world.

38) Most comedy is based on getting a laugh at somebody else's expense. And I find that that's just a form of bullying in a major way. So, I want to be an example of how you can be funny and kind and make people laugh without hurting somebody else's feelings.

39) Sometimes, you can't see yourself clearly until you see yourself through the eyes of others.

40) We focus so much on our differences, which is creating, I think, a lot of chaos, negativity, and bullying in the world. And I think if everybody focused on what we all have in common—which is—we all want to be happy.

41) My dad is still a Christian Scientist. My mom's not, and I'm not. But I believe in God and that there's a higher power and an intelligence that's bigger than us and that we can rely on. It's not just us thinking we are the ones in control of everything. That idea gives me support.

42) While I was doing stand-up, I thought I knew for sure that success meant getting everyone to like me. So, I became whoever I thought people wanted me to be. I'd say yes when I wanted to say no, and I even wore a few dresses. 🏳️‍🌈

43) I'd like to be more patient! I just want everything now. I've tried to meditate, but it's really hard for me to stay still. I'd like to try to force myself to do it because everybody says how wonderful meditation is for you, but I can't shut my mind up. So patience and learning is the key.

44) When we were growing up, our parents somehow made it clear that being famous was good. And I mistakenly thought that if I was famous, then everyone would love me.

45) Right before I decided to come out, I went on a spiritual retreat called 'Changing the Inner Dialogue of Your Subconscious Mind.' I'd never been to anything like it before, and all my friends were taking bets on how long I'd last with no TV, no radio, no phone. But for me, that was the beginning of paying attention to all the little things. 🏳️‍🌈

46) No matter how popular you are as a stand-up—you can go out and fill a 10,000-seat arena and be smart and funny—it's delicate to host an awards show and know where your place is and know that it's not about you, that it's about the people who are nominated and respect that, but at the same time have your moment to show them who you are.

REFERENCES

1) https://en.wikipedia.org/wiki/Ellen_DeGeneres
2) https://www.forbes.com/profile/ellen-degeneres/?sh=5786fbcb3638
3) https://www.ellen-degeneres.com/
4) https://www.gettyimages.com/search/2/image-film?family=creative&phrase=ellen%20degeneres
5) https://www.brainyquote.com/authors/ellen-degeneres-quotes

THANKS FOR READING TILL THE END.

ALL PROCEEDS FROM THIS BOOK WILL BE USED FOR CHARITABLE EFFORTS SUPPORTING THE LESS PRIVILEGED, INTERNALLY DISPLACED PERSONS AND FAMILIES IN SUB-SAHARAN AFRICA

Please stay in touch and let me know your thoughts, questions, comments, concerns, and constructive feedback.

www.fonbertrand.com

www.ingramcontent.com/pod-product-compliance
Lightning Source LLC
Chambersburg PA
CBHW042332150426
43194CB00001B/25